MW00655060

Attract
Wealth

Attract Wealth

Take Charge of Your Life

JOSEPH MURPHY

foreword by **David Cameron Gikandi**
author of *A Happy Pocket Full of Money*

Copyright © 2021 Hampton Roads Publishing
Foreword copyright © 2021 by David Cameron Gikandi
All rights reserved. No part of this publication may be reproduced or
transmitted in any form or by any means, electronic or mechanical, including
photocopying, recording, or by any information storage and retrieval system,
without permission in writing from Red Wheel/Weiser, LLC.
Reviewers may quote brief passages.
Based upon material from *The Power of Your Subconscious Mind.*

Cover and text design by Kathryn Sky-Peck
Typeset in Centaur

Hampton Roads Publishing Company, Inc.
Charlottesville, VA 22906
Distributed by Red Wheel/Weiser, LLC
www.redwheelweiser.com

ISBN: 978-1-64297-033-3

Library of Congress Cataloging-in-Publication Data available upon request.

Printed in the United States of America
IBI

10 9 8 7 6 5 4 3 2 1

Contents

Foreword

In dark and troubled times, we need a light to shine through the darkness and show us the way forward. When we feel helpless and at the mercy of forces that seem beyond our control, when we feel doubtful and worried about our ability to meet even our basic needs, we need to remember there is light within us. And when we think that the only way to meet our needs is to earn more money, which seems harder and harder to do, we need a book like this one to liberate us from the hypnotic spell of fear and scarcity.

This book reminds us of our true source of wealth and abundance. The kingdom is within. In good times, in bad times, even in the bleakest of times, the kingdom is always within. The times do not change that fact. And that is our saving grace.

Joseph Murphy was one of the most important New Thought teachers of the 20th century. He wrote, taught, and lectured widely on consciousness and prosperity. His words remind us that there is just One Invisible Source from which all things flow. The world around you—the plants, the animals, the planets, and even the galaxies—all arose from this Invisible Source. The Universe appeared in one Big Bang from this mysterious Invisible Source. You, too, were birthed from that same Source. That, my friend, is the Kingdom. The power of Life. And it is within you. And it expresses as you, through you, for you.

This mysterious Source gives of itself abundantly, and in accordance with your free will. Ask and it shall be given, seek and you shall find, knock and the door shall be opened to you. Whatever we hold both in our mind and in our emotions, consciously and unconsciously, is automatically given Form and Life by the Source within. In this way, our physical reality acts as a mirror to our consciousness, a perfect design that allows us to truly know ourselves.

The world has taught us, through millennia, to turn away from our True Selves, to forget our own divine creative power, to think of ourselves as mere flesh and bones, as mechanical beings, and that's it. We have been programmed to think of ourselves as insignificant creatures at the mercy of random external forces and that our wealth depends on these external forces.

A person who is unaware of their own spiritual powers falls subject to a mindset of lack and limitation. They fall victim to their fears, their conditioned and limiting thoughts and emotions, to mass unconsciousness. The person that has awakened to their connection to Source becomes a conscious creator, one who doesn't fall prey to the fears of the world, and who is able to meet not just their basic needs, but fulfill their dreams.

Look at the world around you. Notice how nature—Life—is abundant, lavish, extravagant even. Just look. It is all taken care of by Source, with Infinite Intelligence. It is the same with you. Prosperity is an elemental quality of Source, it is an inalienable aspect of your True Nature.

The time has come to let go of the belief that abundance comes *only* from working physically

A person who is
unaware of their own
spiritual powers falls
subject to a mindset of
lack and limitation.

hard for money, that you are at the mercy of a precarious economy or monetary system. It is time to recognize that Source has always been with you, given you life, sustained, and maintained you. As you turn more and more consciously toward Source and away from fear, your ability to think creatively and abundantly will grow in infinite ways as a testament to the infinite Being that you truly are.

Attract Wealth will help you overcome the subconsciously held mental disease of poverty, and to access the infinite riches within you, through aligning your mind and emotions with your divine heritage. Take charge of your life. Claim your right to be rich! Enjoy this little book.

—DAVID CAMERON GIKANDI,
author of *A Happy Pocket Full of Money*

Introduction

Why is one person sad and another happy? Why are some joyous and prosperous and others poor and miserable? Why is one fearful and anxious and another full of faith and confidence? Why does one person have a beautiful, luxurious home while another lives out a meager existence in impoverished conditions? Why is someone a great success and another an abject failure? Why is someone a genius in work or profession while others toil and moil all their lives without doing or accomplishing anything worthwhile? Why is it that so many good, kind, religious people suffer the tortures of the damned in their mind and body? Why is it many immoral and irreligious people succeed and prosper and enjoy abundance and riches? Is there an answer to these questions in the workings of your conscious and subconscious minds?

There most certainly is.

THE REASON FOR WRITING THIS BOOK

It is for the express purpose of answering and clarifying these questions and many others of a similar nature that motivated me to write this book. I have endeavored to explain the great fundamental truths of your mind in the simplest language possible.

I believe that it is perfectly possible to explain the basic, foundational, and fundamental laws of life and of your mind in ordinary everyday language. I urge you to study this book and apply the techniques outlined herein; and as you do, I feel absolutely convinced that you will lay hold of a miracle-working power that will lift you up from confusion, misery, melancholy, and failure. This power will guide you to your true place, solve your difficulties, sever you from emotional and physical bondage, and place you on the royal road to freedom, happiness, peace of mind, and wealth. This miracle-working power of your sub-conscious mind can heal you of what is holding you back, and help you learn to use your inner powers to open the prison door of fear so that you may enter into a life described by Paul as the glorious liberty of the sons of God.

The unique feature of this book is its down-to-earth practicality. Here you are presented with simple, usable techniques and formulas that you can easily apply in your day-to-day

The miracle-working
power of your
subconscious mind can
heal you of what is
holding you back.

world. I have taught these simple processes to men and women all over the world, and recently more than a thousand individuals of all religious affiliations attended a special class in Los Angeles where I presented the highlights of what is offered in the pages of this book. Many came from distances of two hundred miles for each class lesson.

The special features of this book will appeal to you because they show you why oftentimes you get the opposite of what you pray for and will reveal to you the reasons why. People from all corners of the world and from all walks of life have asked me thousands of times, "Why is it I have prayed and prayed and got no answer?"

In this book you will find the reasons for this common complaint. The many ways of impressing the subconscious mind and getting the right answers make this an extraordinarily valuable book and an ever-present help in a time of trouble.

WHAT DO YOU BELIEVE?

It is not the thing believed in that brings an answer to our prayer; the answer to prayer results when the our subconscious mind responds to the mental picture or thought we have in mind.

This law of belief is operating in all religions of the world and is the reason why they are psychologically true. Buddhists, Christians, Muslims, and Jews all may get answers to their prayers, not because of the particular creed, religion, affiliation, ritual, ceremony, formula, liturgy, incantation, sacrifices, or offerings, but solely because of belief or mental acceptance and receptivity about that for which they pray.

The law of life
is the law
of belief.

The law of life is the law of belief, and belief can be summed up briefly as a thought in your mind. As you think, feel, and believe, so is the condition of your mind, body, and circumstances. A technique, a methodology based on an understanding of what you are doing and why you are doing it, will help you to bring about a subconscious embodiment of all the good things of life.

Essentially, answered prayer is the realization of your heart's desire.

Your prayer is answered because your subconscious mind is principle, and by principle I mean the way a thing works. For example, the principle of electricity is that it works from a higher to a lower potential. You do not change the principle of electricity when you use it, but by cooperating with nature, you can bring

Answered prayer is
the realization of your
heart's desire.

forth marvelous inventions and discoveries, which bless humanity in countless ways.

Your subconscious mind is principle and works according to the law of belief. You must know what belief is, why it works, and how it works. The law of your mind is the law of belief. This means you must believe in the way your mind works, to believe in belief itself. The *belief* of your mind is the *thought* of your mind—that is simple—just that and nothing else.

All your experiences, events, conditions, and acts are the reactions of your subconscious mind to your thoughts. Remember, it is not the thing believed in but the belief in your own mind that brings about the result.

Cease believing in the false beliefs, opinions, superstitions, and fears of mankind. Begin to believe in the eternal truths of life, which never change. Then, you will move onward, upward, and Godward.

When you read this book and apply the principles of the subconscious mind herein set forth, you will be able to pray scientifically and effectively for yourself and for others. Your prayer is answered according to the universal law of action and reaction. Thought is incipient action. The reaction is the response from your subconscious mind that corresponds with the nature of your thought.

Busy your mind with the concepts of harmony, health, peace, and good will, and wonders will happen in your life.

chapter one

The Treasure House
Within You

Infinite riches are all around you if you will open your mental eyes and behold the treasure house of infinity within you. There is a gold mine within you from which you can extract everything you need to live life gloriously, joyously, and abundantly.

Many are sound asleep because they do not know about this gold mine of infinite intelligence and boundless love within themselves. Whatever you want, you can draw forth. A magnetized piece of steel will lift about twelve times its own weight, and if you demagnetize this same piece of steel, it will not even lift a feather. Similarly, there are two types of people. One is the magnetized person who is full of confidence and faith. This person knows that he is born to win and to succeed. Then, there is the other type of person who is demagnetized. This person is full of fears and doubts. Opportunities come, and he says, "I might fail; I might lose my money; people will laugh at me." This type of individual will not get very far in life because, if he is afraid to go forward, he will simply stay where he is. Become a magnetized person and discover the master secret of the ages.

THE MASTER SECRET OF THE AGES

What, in your opinion, is the master secret of the ages? The secret of atomic energy? Thermonuclear

energy? The neutron bomb? Interplanetary travel?
No—not any of these. Then, what is this master
secret? Where can one find it, and how can it be
contacted and brought into action? The answer is
extraordinarily simple. This secret is the marvelous, miracle-working power found in your own
subconscious mind, the last place that most people would seek it.

THE MARVELOUS POWER
OF YOUR SUBCONSCIOUS

You can bring into your life more power, more
wealth, more health, more happiness, and more
joy by learning to contact and release the hidden
power of your subconscious mind.

You need not acquire this power; you already
possess it. But, you want to learn how to use it;
you want to understand it so that you can apply
it in all departments of your life.

As you follow the simple techniques and processes set forth in this book, you can gain the necessary knowledge and understanding. A new light can inspire you, and you can generate a new force enabling you to realize your hopes and make all your dreams come true. Decide now to make your life grander, greater, richer, and nobler than ever before.

Within your subconscious depths lie infinite wisdom, infinite power, and an infinite supply of all that is necessary, which is waiting for development and expression. Begin now to recognize these potentialities of your deeper mind, and they will take form in the world without.

The infinite intelligence within your subconscious mind can reveal to you everything you need to know at every moment of time and point in space, provided you are open-minded and receptive. You can receive new thoughts and

Decide now to make
your life grander, greater,
richer, and nobler than
ever before.

ideas enabling you to bring forth new inventions, make new discoveries, or write books and plays. Moreover, the infinite intelligence in your subconscious can impart to you wonderful kinds of knowledge of an original nature. It can reveal to you and open the way for perfect expression and true place in your life.

Through the wisdom of your subconscious mind you can attract prosperity, as well as the right business associate or partner. It can find the right buyer for your home, provide you with all the money you need, and the financial freedom to be, to do, and to go, as your heart desires.

It is your right to discover this inner world of thought, feeling, and power, of light, love, and beauty. Though invisible, its forces are mighty. Within your subconscious mind you will find the solution for every problem, and the cause for every effect. Because you can draw out the hidden powers, you come into actual possession of the power and wisdom necessary to move forward in abundance, security, joy, and dominion.

I have seen the power of the subconscious lift people up out of crippled states, making them whole, vital, and strong once more, and free to go out into the world to experience happiness, health, and joyous expression.

chapter two

How Your Own Mind Works

You have a mind, and you should learn how to use it. There are two levels of your mind: the conscious or rational level, and the subconscious or irrational level. You think with your conscious mind, and whatever you habitually think sinks down into your subconscious mind. And according to the nature of your thoughts, your subconscious mind *creates*. If you think good, good will follow; if you think evil, evil will follow. This is the way your mind works.

The main point to remember is once the subconscious mind accepts an idea, it begins to execute it. It is an interesting and subtle truth that the law of the subconscious mind works for good and bad ideas alike. This law, when applied in a negative way, is the cause of failure, frustration, and unhappiness. However, when your habitual thinking is harmonious and constructive, you experience happiness and prosperity.

Whatever you claim mentally and feel as true, your subconscious mind will accept and bring forth into your experience. The only thing necessary for you to do is to get your subconscious mind to accept your idea, and the law of your own subconscious mind will bring forth what you desire. You give the command or decree, and your subconscious will faithfully reproduce the idea impressed upon it. The law of your mind

According to the nature
of your thoughts, your
subconscious mind
creates.

is this: You will get a reaction or response from your subconscious mind according to the nature of the thought or idea you hold in your conscious mind.

Psychologists and psychiatrists point out that when thoughts are conveyed to your subconscious mind, impressions are made in the brain cells. As soon as your subconscious accepts any idea, it proceeds to put it into effect immediately. It works by association of ideas and uses every bit of knowledge that you have gathered in your lifetime to bring about its purpose. It draws on the infinite power, energy, and wisdom within you. It lines up all the laws of nature to get its way. Sometimes it seems to bring about an immediate solution to your difficulties, but at other times it may take days, weeks, or longer. Its ways are mysterious and past finding out.

CONSCIOUS AND SUBCONSCIOUS TERMS
DIFFERENTIATED

Your conscious and subconscious mind are not two minds. They are merely two spheres of activity within one mind. Your conscious mind is the reasoning mind. It is the phase of mind that chooses. For example, you choose your books, your home, and your partner in life. You make all your decisions with your conscious mind.

On the other hand, without any conscious choice on your part, your heart is kept functioning automatically, and the process of digestion, circulation, and breathing are carried on by your subconscious mind through processes independent of your conscious control.

Your subconscious mind accepts what is impressed upon it or what you consciously believe. It does not reason things out like your conscious mind, and it does not argue with you.

Your subconscious mind is like the soil, which accepts any kind of seed, good or bad. Your thoughts are active and might be likened unto seeds. Negative, destructive thoughts continue to work negatively in your subconscious mind, and in due time will come forth into outer experience that corresponds with them.

Remember, your subconscious mind does not engage in proving whether your thoughts are good or bad, true or false, but it responds according to the nature of your thoughts or suggestions. For example, if you consciously assume something as true, even though it may be false, your subconscious mind will accept it as true and proceed to bring about results, which must necessarily follow, because you consciously assumed it to be true.

THE TERMS *OBJECTIVE MIND* AND *SUBJECTIVE MIND* CLARIFIED

Your conscious mind is sometimes referred to as your objective mind because it deals with outward objects. The objective mind takes cognizance of the objective world. Its media of observation are your five physical senses. Your objective mind is your guide and director in your contact with your environment. You gain knowledge through your five senses. Your objective mind learns through observation, experience, and education. As previously pointed out, the greatest function of the objective mind is that of reasoning.

Suppose you are one of the thousands of tourists who come to Los Angeles annually. You would come to the conclusion that it is a beautiful city based upon your observation of the parks, pretty gardens, majestic buildings, and lovely homes. This is the working of your objective mind.

Your subconscious mind is oftentimes referred to as your subjective mind. Your subjective mind takes cognizance of its environment by means independent of the five senses. Your subjective mind perceives by intuition.

It is the seat of your emotion and the storehouse of memory. Your subjective mind performs its highest functions when your objective senses are in abeyance. In a word, it is that intelligence which makes itself manifest when the objective mind is suspended or in a sleepy, drowsy state.

Your subjective mind sees without the use of the natural organs of vision. Let's take the same example of visiting Los Angeles, although you've heard it's an awful city, smoggy and full of crime. When you visit the city, that is what you will see; that experience is the seed that had been planted.

It is of the greatest importance that we understand the interaction of the objective and subjective mind in order to learn the true art of prayer.

THE SUBCONSCIOUS CANNOT REASON LIKE YOUR CONSCIOUS MIND

Your subconscious mind cannot argue controversially. If you give it wrong suggestions, it will accept them as true and will proceed to bring them to pass as conditions, experiences, and events. All things that have happened to you are based on thoughts impressed on your subconscious mind through belief. If you have conveyed erroneous concepts to your subconscious mind, the only sure method of overcoming them is by the repetition of constructive, harmonious thoughts frequently repeated. These your subconscious mind accepts, and thus forms new and healthy habits of thought and life. Your subconscious mind is the seat of habit.

The habitual thinking of your conscious mind establishes deep grooves in your subconscious mind. This is very favorable for you if your habitual thoughts are harmonious, peaceful, and constructive. But if you have consciously indulged in fear, worry, and other destructive forms of thinking, the remedy is to recognize the omnipotence of your subconscious mind and decree freedom, happiness, and abundance. Your subconscious mind, being creative and one with your divine source, will proceed to create that which you have earnestly decreed.

THE TREMENDOUS POWER
OF SUGGESTION

Your conscious mind is the "watchman at the gate," and its chief function is to protect your subconscious mind from false impressions.

Your subconscious mind is amenable to suggestion. As you know, your subconscious mind does not make comparisons, or contrasts, neither does it reason and think things out for itself. This latter function belongs to your conscious mind. It simply reacts to the impressions given to it by your conscious mind. It does not show a preference for one course of action over another.

You must still the wheels of your mind, relax, let go, and quietly affirm the art of prayer: the synchronized, harmonious, and intelligent function of the conscious and subconscious levels of mind specifically directed for a definite purpose.

chapter three

How to Get the Results You Want

The principle reasons for failure are: lack of confidence and too much effort. Many people block answers to their prayers by failing to fully comprehend the workings of their subconscious mind.

When you know how your mind functions, you gain a measure of confidence. You must remember whenever your subconscious mind accepts an idea, it immediately begins to execute it. It uses all its mighty resources to that end and mobilizes all the mental and spiritual laws of your deeper mind. This law is true for good or bad ideas. Consequently, if you use it negatively, it brings trouble, failure, and confusion. When you use it constructively, it brings guidance, freedom, and peace of mind.

The right answer is inevitable when your thoughts are positive, constructive, and loving. From this it is perfectly obvious that the only thing you have to do in order to overcome failure is to get your subconscious to accept your idea or request by feeling its reality now, and the law of your mind will do the rest. Turn over your request with faith and confidence, and your subconscious will take over and answer for you.

You will always fail to get results by trying to use mental coercion—your subconscious mind does not respond to coercion, it responds to your faith or conscious mind acceptance.

You must remember
whenever your
subconscious mind
accepts an idea, it
immediately begins to
execute it.

Your failure to get results may also arise from such statements as: "Things are getting worse." "I will never get an answer." "I see no way out." "It's hopeless." "I don't know what to do." "I'm all mixed up." When you use such statements, you get no response or cooperation from your subconscious mind. Like a soldier marking time, you neither go forward nor backward; in other words, you don't get anywhere.

If you get into a taxi and give half a dozen different directions to the driver in five minutes, he will become hopelessly confused and probably refuse to take you anywhere. It is the same when working with your subconscious mind. You must have a clear-cut idea in your mind. You must arrive at the definite decision that there is a way out, a solution to the vexing problem. Only the infinite intelligence within your subconscious knows the answer. When you come to that clear-cut conclusion in your conscious mind, your mind is then made up, and according to your belief is it done unto you.

EASY DOES IT

A house owner once remonstrated with a furnace repairman for charging two hundred dollars for fixing the boiler. The mechanic said, "I charged five cents for the missing bolt and one hundred ninety-nine dollars and ninety-five cents for knowing what was wrong."

Similarly, your subconscious mind is the master mechanic, the all-wise one, who knows ways and means of achieving your goals, as well as your affairs. Decree wealth, and your subconscious will establish it. But relaxation is the key: "Easy does it." Do not be concerned with details and means, but know the end result. Get the feel of the happy solution to your problem whether it is wealth, health, or employment. Bear in mind that your feeling is the touchstone of all subconscious demonstration. Your new idea must be felt subjectively in a finished state, not in the future, but as coming about *now*.

INFER NO OPPONENT; USE IMAGINATION AND NOT WILL POWER

In using your subconscious mind you infer no opponent, you use no will power. You imagine the end and the freedom state. You will find your intellect trying to get in the way, but persist in maintaining a simple, childlike, miracle-making faith. Picture yourself without the roadblock or problem. Imagine the state of freedom and wealth you crave. Cut out all red tape from the process. The simple way is the best.

Persist in maintaining
a simple, childlike,
miracle-making faith.

HOW DISCIPLINED IMAGINATION
WORKS WONDERS

A wonderful way to get a response from your subconscious mind is through disciplined or scientific imagination. As previously pointed out, your subconscious mind is the builder of the body and controls all its vital functions.

The Bible says, *whatsoever ye shall ask in prayer, believing, ye shall receive.* To believe is to accept something as true, or to live in the state of being it. As you sustain this mood, you shall experience the joy of the answered prayer!

The three steps to success in prayer
The usual procedure is as follows:

1. Take a look at the problem.
2. Turn to the solution or way out known only to the subconscious mind.
3. Rest in a sense of deep conviction that it is done.

Do not weaken your prayer by saying, "I *wish* I *might* be healed," or "I *hope* so." Your feeling about the work to be done is "the boss." Harmony is yours. Know that abundance is yours. Become intelligent by becoming a vehicle for the infinite power of the subconscious mind. Pass on the idea of wealth to your subconscious mind to the point of conviction; then relax. Get yourself off your hands. Say to the condition and circumstance, "This, too, shall pass." Through relaxation you impress your subconscious mind, enabling the kinetic energy behind the idea to take over and bring it into concrete realization.

THE LAW OF REVERSED EFFORT AND WHY YOU GET THE OPPOSITE OF WHAT YOU PRAY FOR

Emile Coué (1857–1926) was a French psychologist who introduced the notion of self-improvement based on optimistic suggestion.

Pass on the idea
of wealth to your
subconscious mind
to the point
of conviction;
then relax.

He most famously came up with the mantra, "Every day, in every way, I'm getting better and better." Coué defined the law of reversed effort as follows: "When your desires and imagination are in conflict your imagination invariably gains the day."

If, for example, you were asked to walk a plank on the floor, you would do so without question. Now suppose the same plank were placed twenty feet up in the air between two walls—would you walk it? Your desire to walk it would be counteracted by your imagination or fear of falling. Your dominant idea, which would be the picture of falling, would conquer. Your desire, will, or effort to walk on the plank would be reversed, and the dominant idea of failure would be reinforced.

Mental effort is invariably self-defeated, eventuating always in the opposite of what is desired. The suggestions of powerlessness to overcome the condition dominate the mind; your subconscious is always controlled by the dominant idea. Your subconscious will accept the stronger of two contradictory propositions. The effortless way is the better way.

If you say, "I want a healing, but I can't get it," or "I try so hard," or "I force myself to pray," or "I use all the willpower I have," then you must realize that your error lies in your effort. Never try to compel the subconscious mind to accept your idea by exercising willpower. Such attempts are doomed to failure, and you get the opposite of what you prayed for.

The following is a rather common experience. Students, when taking examinations and reading through their papers, often find that all their knowledge has suddenly deserted them. Their minds become appalling blanks, and they are unable to recall one relevant thought. The more they grit their teeth and summon the powers of the will, the further the answers seem to flee. But, when they have left the examination room and the mental pressure relaxes, the answers they were seeking flow tantalizingly back into their minds.

Trying to force themselves to remember was the cause of their failure. This is an example of the law of reversed effort whereby you get the opposite of what you asked or prayed for.

THE CONFLICT OF DESIRE AND IMAGINATION MUST BE RECONCILED

To use mental force is to presuppose that there is opposition. When your mind is concentrated on the *means* to overcome a problem, it is no longer concerned with the obstacle. Matthew 18:19 says, *If two of you shall agree on earth as touching anything that they shall ask, it shall be done for them of my Father which is in heaven.*

Who are these two?

It means the harmonious union or agreement between your conscious and subconscious on any idea, desire, or mental image. When there is no longer any quarrel in either part of your mind, your prayer will be answered. The two agreeing may also be represented as you and your desire, your thought and feeling, your idea and emotion, your desire and imagination.

You can avoid all conflict between your desires and imagination by entering into a drowsy, sleepy state; this brings all effort to a minimum.

The conscious mind is submerged to a great extent when in a sleepy state.

The best time to impregnate your subconscious is prior to sleep. The reason for this is that the highest degree of outcropping of the subconscious occurs prior to sleep and just after we awaken. In this state, the negative thoughts and imagery, which tend to neutralize your desire and so prevent acceptance by your subconscious mind, no longer present themselves. When you imagine the reality of the fulfilled desire and feel the thrill of accomplishment, your subconscious brings about the realization of your desire.

A great many people solve all their dilemmas and problems by the play of their controlled, directed, and disciplined imagination, knowing that whatever they imagine and feel as true will and must come to pass.

The following will clearly illustrate how a woman overcame the conflict between her desire and her imagination. She desired a harmonious solution to her legal problem, yet her mental imagery was constantly on failure, loss, bankruptcy, and poverty. She was involved in a complicated lawsuit and there was one postponement after another with no solution in sight.

At my suggestion, she got into a sleepy, drowsy state each night prior to sleep, and she began to imagine the happy ending, feeling it to the best of her ability. She knew that the image in her mind had to agree with her heart's desire.

Prior to sleep, she began to dramatize as vividly as possible her lawyer having an animated discussion with her regarding the outcome. She would ask him questions, and he would answer her appropriately. He would say to her over and over again, "There has been a perfect, harmonious solution. The case has been settled out of court."

During the day, when fear thoughts came into her mind, she would run her mental movie with gestures, voice, and sound equipment. She could easily imagine the sound of his voice, smile, and mannerisms. She ran this mental picture so often; it became a subjective pattern, a regular train track.

At the end of a few weeks her attorney called her and confirmed objectively what she had been imagining and feeling as true subjectively.

This is really what the Psalmist meant when he wrote, *Let the words of my mouth [your thoughts, mental images, good] and the meditations of my heart [your feeling, nature, emotion] be acceptable in thy sight, O Lord [the law of your subconscious mind], my strength, and my redeemer [the power and wisdom of your subconscious mind can redeem you from sickness, bondage, and misery]. Psalm 19:14.*

- Mental coercion or too much effort shows anxiety and fear, which block your answer. Easy does it.

- When your mind is relaxed and you accept an idea, your subconscious goes to work to execute the idea.

- Think and plan independently of traditional methods. Know that there is always an answer and a solution to every problem.

- Do not be overly concerned with the beating of your heart, with the breathing of your lungs, or the functions of any part of your anatomy. Lean heavily upon your subconscious and proclaim frequently that Divine right action is taking place.

- The feeling of health produces health;
  the feeling of wealth produces wealth.
  How do you feel?
- Imagination is your most powerful
  faculty. Imagine what is lovely and
  of good report. You are what you
  imagine yourself to be.
- You avoid conflict between your
  conscious and subconscious in the
  sleepy state. Imagine the fulfillment of
  your desire over and over again prior to
  sleep. Sleep in peace and wake in joy.

chapter four

How to Use the Power of Your Subconscious for Wealth

If you are having financial difficulties, if you are trying to make ends meet, it means you have not convinced your subconscious mind that you will always have plenty and some to spare. You know men and women who work a few hours a week and make fabulous sums of money. They do not strive or slave hard. Do not believe the story that the only way you can become wealthy is by the sweat of your brow and hard labor. It is not so; the effortless way of life is the best. Do the thing you love to do, and do it for the joy and thrill of it.

I know an executive in Los Angeles who receives an enormous salary yearly. Last year he went on a nine-month cruise to see the world and its beauty spots. He said to me that he had succeeded in convincing his subconscious mind that he is worth that much money. He told me that many people in his organization getting less money per week actually knew more about the business than he did, and could manage it better, but they had no ambition, no creative ideas, and were not interested in the wonders of their subconscious mind.

WEALTH IS OF THE MIND

Wealth is simply a subconscious conviction on the part of the individual.

You will not become a millionaire by saying, "I am a millionaire, I am a millionaire." You will grow into a wealth consciousness by building into your mentality the idea of wealth and abundance.

YOUR INVISIBLE MEANS OF SUPPORT

The trouble with most people is that they have no invisible means of support. When business falls away, the stock market drops, or they lose their investments, they seem helpless. The reason for such insecurity is that they do not know how to tap the subconscious mind. They are unacquainted with the inexhaustible storehouse within.

A man with a poverty-type mind finds himself in poverty-stricken conditions. Another man with a mind filled with ideas of wealth is surrounded with everything he needs. It was never intended that man should lead a life of

Wealth is simply a
subconscious conviction
on the part of the
individual.

indigence. You can have wealth, everything you need, and plenty to spare. Your words have power to cleanse your mind of wrong ideas and to instill right ideas in their place.

THE IDEAL METHOD FOR BUILDING A WEALTH CONSCIOUSNESS

Perhaps you are saying as you read this chapter, "I need wealth and success." This is what you do: Repeat for about five minutes to yourself three or four times a day, "Wealth—Success." These words have tremendous power. They represent the inner power of the subconscious mind. Anchor your mind on this substantial power within you; then conditions and circumstances corresponding to their nature and quality will be manifested in your life.

You are not saying, "I am wealthy"; you are dwelling on real powers within you. There is no

conflict in the mind when you say, "Wealth."
Furthermore, the feeling of wealth will well up
within you as you dwell on the idea of wealth.

The feeling of wealth produces wealth; keep
this in mind at all times. Your subconscious
mind is like a bank, a sort of universal financial
institution. It magnifies whatever you deposit or
impress upon it whether it is the idea of wealth
or of poverty. Choose wealth.

WHY YOUR AFFIRMATIONS
FOR WEALTH FAIL

I have talked to many people during the past
thirty-five years whose usual complaint is, "I
have said for weeks and months, 'I am wealthy,
I am prosperous,' and nothing has happened."
I discovered that when they said, "I am prosperous, I am wealthy," they felt within that they
were lying to themselves.

The feeling of wealth
produces wealth;
keep this in mind
at all times.

One man told me, "I have repeated the affirmation that I am prosperous to the point of tiring myself out. Things are now worse. I knew when I made the statement that it was obviously not true." His statements were rejected by the conscious mind, and the very opposite of what he outwardly affirmed and claimed was made manifest.

Your affirmation succeeds best when it is specific and when it does not produce a mental conflict or argument; hence the statements made by this man made matters worse because they suggested his lack. Your subconscious accepts what you really feel to be true, not just idle words or statements. The dominant idea or belief is always accepted by the subconscious mind.

HOW TO AVOID MENTAL CONFLICT

The following is the ideal way to overcome this conflict for those who have this difficulty. Make this practical statement frequently, particularly prior to sleep: "By day and by night I am being prospered in all of my interests." This affirmation will not arouse any argument because it does not contradict your subconscious mind's impression of financial lack.

I suggested to one businessman whose sales and finances were very low and who was greatly worried, that he sit down in his office, become quiet, and repeat this statement over and over again: "My sales are improving every day." This statement engaged the cooperation of the conscious and subconscious mind; results followed.

DON'T SIGN BLANK CHECKS

You sign blank checks when you make such statements as, "There is not enough to go around." "There is a shortage." "I will lose the house because of the mortgage." If you are full of fear about the future, you are also writing a blank check and attracting negative conditions to you. Your subconscious mind takes your fear and negative statement as your request and proceeds in its own way to bring obstacles, delays, lack, and limitation into your life.

YOUR SUBCONSCIOUS GIVES YOU COMPOUND INTEREST

To him that hath the feeling of wealth, more wealth shall be added; to him that hath the feeling of lack, more lack shall be added. Your subconscious multiplies and magnifies whatever you deposit in it. Every morning as you awaken,

If you convince your
subconscious mind that
wealth is yours, that
it is always circulating
in your life, you will
always and inevitably
have it, regardless of
the form it takes.

deposit thoughts of prosperity, success, wealth, and peace. Dwell upon these concepts. Busy your mind with them as often as possible. These constructive thoughts will find their way as deposits in your subconscious mind, and bring forth abundance and prosperity.

WHY NOTHING HAPPENED

I can hear you saying, "Oh, I did that and nothing happened." You did not get results because you indulged in fear thoughts perhaps ten minutes later and neutralized the good you had affirmed. When you place a seed in the ground, you do not dig it up. You let it take root and grow.

Suppose, for example, you are going to say, "I won't be able to make that payment." Before you get further than, "I won't—" stop the sentence and dwell on a constructive statement, such as, "By day and by night I prosper in all my ways."

TRUE SOURCE OF WEALTH

Your subconscious mind is never short of ideas. There are within it an infinite number of ideas ready to flow into your conscious mind and appear as cash in your pocketbook in countless ways. This process will continue to go on in your mind regardless of whether the stock market goes up or down, or whether the dollar or Euro drops in value. Your wealth is never truly dependent on bonds, stocks, or money in the bank; these are really only symbols. Necessary and useful, of course, but only symbols.

The point I wish to emphasize is that if you convince your subconscious mind that wealth is yours, and that it is always circulating in your life, you will always and inevitably have it, regardless of the form it takes.

chapter five

A Common
Stumbling Block
to Wealth

There are people who claim that they are always trying to make ends meet. They seem to have a great struggle to meet their obligations. Have you listened to their conversation? In many instances their conversation runs along this vein: They are constantly condemning those who have succeeded in life and who have raised their heads above the crowd. Perhaps they say, "Oh, that fellow has a racket; he is ruthless; he is a crook." This is why they lack; they are condemning the thing they desire and want. The reason they speak critically of their more prosperous associates is because they are envious and covetous of the others' prosperity. The quickest way to cause wealth to take wing and fly away is to criticize and condemn others who have more wealth than you.

There is one emotion that is the cause of the lack of wealth in the lives of many. Most people learn this the hard way. It is envy. For example, if you see a competitor depositing large sums of money in the bank, and you have only a meager amount to deposit, does it make you envious? The way to overcome this emotion is to say to yourself, "Isn't it wonderful! I rejoice in that man's prosperity. I wish for him greater and greater wealth."

The quickest way to
cause wealth to take
wing and fly away is to
criticize and condemn
others who have more
wealth than you.

To entertain envious thoughts is devastating because it places you in a very negative position; therefore, wealth flows from you instead of to you. If you are ever annoyed or irritated by the prosperity or great wealth of another, claim immediately that you truly wish for him greater wealth in every possible way. This will neutralize the negative thoughts in your mind and cause an ever-greater measure of wealth to flow to you by the law of your own subconscious mind.

RUBBING OUT A GREAT MENTAL BLOCK TO WEALTH

If you are worried and critical about someone whom you claim is making money dishonestly, cease worrying about him. You know such a person is using the law of mind negatively; the law of mind takes care of him. Be careful not to criticize him for the reasons previously indicated.

Remember: The block or obstacle to wealth is in your own mind. You can now destroy that mental block. This you may do by getting on mental good terms with everyone.

chapter six

Sleep and Grow Rich

As you go to sleep at night, practice the following technique. Repeat the word "Wealth" quietly, easily, and feelingly. Do this over and over again, just like a lullaby. Lull yourself to sleep with the one word, "Wealth." You will be amazed at the result. Wealth should flow to you in avalanches of abundance. This is another example of the magic power of your subconscious mind.

SERVE YOURSELF WITH THE
POWERS OF YOUR MIND

Decide to be wealthy the easy way, with the infallible aid of your subconscious mind.

Trying to accumulate wealth by the sweat of your brow and hard labor is one way to become the richest man in the graveyard. You do not have to strive or slave hard.

Wealth is a subconscious conviction. Build into your mentality the idea of wealth.

The trouble with most people is that they have no invisible means of support.

Repeat the word "Wealth" to yourself slowly and quietly for about five minutes prior to sleep and your subconscious will bring wealth to pass in your experience.

The feeling of wealth produces wealth. Keep this in mind at all times.

Wealth is a
subconscious
conviction. Build into
your mentality the
idea of wealth.

Your conscious and subconscious mind must agree. Your subconscious accepts what you really feel to be true. The dominant idea is always accepted by your subconscious mind. The dominant idea should be wealth, not poverty.

You can overcome any mental conflict regarding wealth by affirming frequently, "By day and by night I am being prospered in all of my interests."

Increase your sales by repeating this statement over and over again: "My sales are improving every day; I am advancing, progressing, and getting wealthier every day."

Stop writing blank checks, such as, "There is not enough to go around," or "There is a shortage." Such statements magnify and multiply your loss.

Deposit thoughts of prosperity, wealth, and success in your subconscious mind, and the latter will give you compound interest.

What you consciously affirm, you must not mentally deny a few moments later. This will neutralize the good you have affirmed.

Your true source of wealth consists of the ideas in your mind. You can have an idea worth millions of dollars. Your subconscious will give you the idea you seek.

Envy and jealousy are stumbling blocks to the flow of wealth. Rejoice in the prosperity of others.

The block to wealth is in your own mind. Destroy that block now by getting on good mental terms with everyone.

chapter seven

Your Right to
Be Rich

It is your right to be rich. You are here to lead
the abundant life and be happy, radiant, and
free. You should, therefore, have all the money
you need to lead a full, happy, and prosperous
life.

You are here to grow, expand, and unfold
spiritually, mentally, and materially. You have
the inalienable right to fully develop and express
yourself along all lines. You should surround
yourself with beauty and luxury.

Why be satisfied with just enough to go around when you can enjoy the riches of your subconscious mind? In this chapter you can learn to make friends with money, and you should always have a surplus. Your desire to be rich is a desire for a fuller, happier, more wonderful life. It is a cosmic urge. It is not only good, but also very good.

MONEY IS A SYMBOL

Money is a symbol of exchange. It means to you not only freedom from want, but beauty, luxury, abundance, and refinement. It is merely a symbol of the economic health of the nation. When your blood is circulating freely in your body, you are healthy. When money is circulating freely in your life, you are economically healthy. When people begin to hoard money, to put it away in tin boxes, and become charged with fear, there is economic illness.

Money has taken many forms as a medium of exchange down through the centuries, such as salt, beads, and trinkets of various kinds. In early times a person's wealth was determined by the number of sheep and oxen he had. Now we use currency, and other negotiable instruments, as it is much more convenient to write a check than carry some sheep around with you to pay bills.

HOW TO WALK THE ROYAL ROAD TO RICHES

Knowledge of the powers of your subconscious mind is the means to the royal road to riches of all kinds—spiritual, mental, or financial. The student of the laws of mind believes and knows definitely that, regardless of economic situations, stock market fluctuation, depression, strikes, war, and other conditions or circumstances, he will always be amply supplied,

Knowledge of the
powers of your
subconscious mind
is the means to
the royal road to
riches of all kinds—
spiritual, mental, or
financial.

regardless of what form money takes. The reason for this is that he has conveyed the idea of wealth to his subconscious mind, and it keeps him supplied wherever he may be. He has convinced himself in his mind that money is forever flowing freely in his life and that there is always a wonderful surplus. Should there be a financial collapse of government tomorrow and all the man's present holdings become valueless, as the German marks did after the First World War, he would still attract wealth and be cared for, regardless of the form the new currency took.

WHY YOU DO NOT HAVE MORE MONEY

As you read this chapter, you are probably saying, "I am worthy of a higher salary than I am receiving." I believe most people are inadequately compensated. One of the reasons many people do not have more money is that they are silently or openly condemning it. They refer to money as "filthy lucre" or "the love of money is the root of all evil." Another reason they do not prosper is that they have a sneaky subconscious feeling there is some virtue in poverty. This subconscious pattern may be due to early childhood training or superstition, or it could be based on a false interpretation of scriptures.

MONEY AND A BALANCED LIFE

One time a man said to me, "I am broke. I do not like money. It is the root of all evil." These statements represent a confused neurotic mind. Love of money to the exclusion of everything else will cause you to become lopsided and unbalanced. You are here to use your power or authority wisely. Some men crave power; others crave money.

If you set your heart on money exclusively and say, "Money is all I want; I am going to give all my attention to amassing money; nothing else matters," you can get money and attain a fortune, but you have forgotten that you are here to lead a balanced life. You must also satisfy the hunger for peace of mind, harmony, love, joy, and perfect health.

By making money your sole aim, you simply made a wrong choice. You thought that was all you wanted, but you found after all your efforts that it was not only the money you needed. You also desired true expression of your hidden talents, true place in life, beauty, and the joy of contributing to the welfare and success of others.

By learning the laws of your subconscious mind, you could have a million dollars or many millions if you wanted them, and still have peace of mind, harmony, perfect health, and perfect expression.

WHY YOU MUST NEVER CRITICIZE MONEY

There is no virtue in poverty; it is a disease like any other mental disease. If you were physically ill, you would think there was something wrong with you. You would seek help and do something about the condition at once. Likewise, if you do not have money constantly circulating in your life, there is something radically wrong with you.

The urge of the life principle in you is toward growth, expansion, and a more abundant life. You are not here to live in a hovel, dress in rags, and go hungry. You should be happy, prosperous, and successful.

There is no virtue
in poverty; it is a
disease like any
other mental disease.

Cleanse your mind of all weird and superstitious beliefs about money. Do not ever regard money as evil or filthy. If you do, you cause it to take wings and fly away from you. Remember that you lose what you condemn. You cannot attract what you criticize.

GETTING THE RIGHT ATTITUDE TOWARD MONEY

Here is a simple technique you may use to multiply money in your experience. Use the following statements several times a day: "I like money, I love it, I use it wisely, constructively, and judiciously. Money is constantly circulating in my life. I release it with joy, and it returns to me multiplied in a wonderful way. It is good and very good. Money flows to me in avalanches of abundance. I use it for good only, and I am grateful for my good and for the riches of my mind."

HOW THE SCIENTIFIC THINKER
LOOKS AT MONEY

Suppose, for example, you found gold, silver, lead, copper, or iron in the ground. Would you pronounce these things evil? All evil comes from our darkened understanding, from our ignorance, from our false interpretation of life, and from our misuse of our subconscious mind.

Uranium, lead, or some other metal could have been used as a medium of exchange. We use paper bills, checks, nickel, and silver—surely these are not evil. Physicists and chemists know today that the only difference between one metal and another is the number and rate of motion of electrons revolving around a central nucleus. They can now change one metal into another through a bombardment of the atoms in the powerful cyclotron. Gold under certain conditions becomes mercury. I believe that our

Remember that you lose
what you condemn.
You cannot attract what
you criticize.

modern scientists in the near future will be able to make gold, silver, and other metals synthetically in the chemical laboratory. The cost may be prohibitive now, but it can be done. I cannot imagine any intelligent person seeing anything evil in electrons, neutrons, protons, and isotopes.

The piece of paper in your pocket is composed of atoms and molecules with their electrons and protons arranged differently. Their number and rate of motion are different. That is the only way the paper differs from the coins in your pocket.

chapter eight

How to Attract the Wealth You Need

Many years ago I met a young boy in Australia who wanted to become a physician and surgeon but he had no money. I explained to him how a seed deposited in the soil attracts to itself everything necessary for its unfolding, and that all he had to do was to take a lesson from the seed and deposit the required idea in his subconscious mind.

For expenses, this young, brilliant boy used to clean out doctors' offices, wash windows, and do odd repair jobs. He told me that every night as he went to sleep, he used to picture in his mind's eye a medical diploma on a wall with his name on it in big, bold letters.

He used to clean and shine the framed diplomas in the medical building where he worked. It was not hard for him to engrave the image of a diploma in his mind and develop it there. Definite results followed as he persisted with his mental picture every night for about four months.

The second part of this story is very interesting. One of the doctors took a great liking to this young boy and after training him in the art of sterilizing instruments, giving hypodermic injections, and other miscellaneous first-aid work, he employed him as a technical assistant in his office. The doctor later sent him to medical school at his own expense.

Having seen the
end result in your
subconscious mind,
you have willed the
means to the realization
of that end.

Today, this young man is a prominent medical doctor in Montreal. He discovered the law of attraction by using his subconscious mind the right way. He operated an age-old law that says, "Having seen the end, you have willed the means to the realization of the end." The end in this case was to become a medical doctor.

This young man was able to imagine, see, and feel the reality of being a doctor. He lived with that idea, sustained it, nourished it, and loved it until through his imagination it penetrated the layers of his subconscious mind and became a conviction, thereby attracting to him everything necessary for the fulfillment of his dream.

WHY SOME DO NOT GET A RAISE IN PAY

If you are working in a large organization and you are silently thinking of and resenting the fact you are underpaid, that you are not appreciated, and that you deserve more money and greater recognition, you are subconsciously severing your ties with that organization. You are setting a law in motion, and the superintendent or manager will say to you, "We have to let you go."

Actually, you dismissed yourself. The manager was simply the instrument through which your own negative mental state was confirmed. It was an example of the law of action and reaction. The action was your thought, and the reaction was the response of your subconscious mind.

OBSTACLES AND IMPEDIMENTS ON THE PATHWAY TO RICHES

I am sure you have heard people say, "That fellow has a racket." "He is a racketeer." "He is getting money dishonestly." "He is a faker."

"I knew him when he had nothing." "He is a crook, a thief, and a swindler."

If you analyze the person who talks like that, you discover he is usually in want or suffering from some financial or physical illness. Perhaps his former college friends went up the ladder of success and left him behind. Now he is bitter and envious of the other fellows' progress. In many instances, this is the cause of his downfall. Thinking negatively of these classmates and condemning their wealth causes the wealth and prosperity he is praying for to vanish and flee. He is condemning the thing he is praying for.

He is praying two ways. On the one hand he is saying, "Wealth is flowing to me now," and in the next breath, silently or audibly, he is saying, "I resent that fellow's wealth." Always make it a special point to rejoice in the wealth of the other person.

PROTECT YOUR INVESTMENTS

If you are seeking wisdom regarding investments, or if you are worried about your stocks
or bonds, quietly claim, "Infinite intelligence
governs and watches over all my financial transactions, and whatsoever I do shall prosper."
Do this frequently and you will find that your
investments will be wise; moreover, you will be
protected from loss, as you will be prompted to
sell your securities or holdings before any loss
accrues to you.

YOU CANNOT GET SOMETHING
FOR NOTHING

In large stores the management employs security
guards to prevent people from stealing. They
catch a number of people every day trying to
get something for nothing. All such people are
living in the mental atmosphere of lack and

Quietly claim,
"Infinite intelligence
governs and watches
over all my financial
transactions, and
whatsoever I do
shall prosper."

limitation and are stealing from themselves peace, harmony, faith, honesty, integrity, good will, and confidence. Furthermore, they are attracting to themselves all manner of loss, such as loss of character, prestige, social status, and peace of mind. These people lack faith in the source of supply and the understanding of how their minds work. If they would mentally call on the powers of their subconscious mind and claim that they are guided to their true expression, they would find work and constant supply. Then by honesty, integrity, and perseverance, they would become a credit to themselves and to society at large.

chapter nine

Your Constant Supply
of Wealth

Recognizing the powers of your subconscious mind and the creative power of your thought or mental image is the way to opulence, freedom, and constant supply. Accept the abundant life in your own mind. Your mental acceptance and expectancy of wealth has its own mathematics and mechanics of expression. As you enter into the mood of opulence, all things necessary for the abundant life will come to pass.

Let this be your daily affirmation; write in your heart, "I am one with the infinite riches of

Accept the abundant life
in your own mind.

my subconscious mind. It is my right to be rich, happy, and successful. Money flows to me freely, copiously, and endlessly. I am forever conscious of my true worth. I give of my talents freely, and I am wonderfully blessed financially. It is wonderful!"

STEP UP THIS WAY TO RICHES

- Be bold enough to claim that it is your right to be rich and your deeper mind will honor your claim.
- You don't want just enough to go around. You want all the money you need to do all the things you want to do and when you want to do them. Get acquainted with the riches of your subconscious mind.
- When money is circulating freely in your life, you are economically healthy.

Be bold enough to claim
that it is your right
to be rich.

Look at money like the tide and you will always have plenty of it. The ebb and flow of the tide is constant. When the tide is out, you are absolutely sure that it will return.

- Knowing the laws of your subconscious mind, you will always be supplied regardless of what form money takes.

- One reason many people simply make ends meet and never have enough money is that they condemn money. What you condemn takes wings and flies away.

- Do not make a god of money. It is only a symbol. Remember that the real riches are in your mind. You are here to lead a balanced life—this includes acquiring all the money you need.

- Don't make money your sole aim. Claim wealth, happiness, peace, true expression, and love, and personally radiate love and good will to all. Then your subconscious mind will give you compound interest in all these fields of expression.

- There is no virtue in poverty. It is a disease of the mind, and you should heal yourself of this mental conflict or malady at once.

- You are not here to live in a hovel, to dress in rags, or to go hungry. You are here to lead the life more abundant.

- Never use the terms "filthy lucre" or "I despise money." You lose what you criticize. There is nothing good or bad, but thinking of it in either light makes it so.

- Repeat frequently, "I like money. I use it wisely, constructively, and judiciously. I release it with joy, and it returns a thousand fold."

As you enter into the mood of opulence, all things necessary for the abundant life will come to pass.

- Money is not evil any more so than copper, lead, tin, or iron that you may find in the ground. All evil is due to ignorance and misuse of the mind's powers.
- To picture the end result in your mind causes your subconscious to respond and fulfill your mental picture.
- Stop trying to get something for nothing. There is no such thing as a free lunch. You must give to receive. You must give mental attention to your goals, ideals, and enterprises, and your deeper mind will back you up. The key to wealth is application of the laws of the subconscious mind by impregnating it with the idea of wealth.

"I am one with the infinite riches of my subconscious mind. It is my right to be rich, happy, and successful."

About the Author

D r. Joseph Murphy (1898–1981) was a leading proponent of the New Thought movement, which developed in the late 19th and early 20th centuries by philosophers and deep thinkers who advocated and practiced a new way of looking at life and obtaining desires. Acclaimed as a major figure in the human potential movement, Murphy has been seen as the spiritual heir to writers like Napoleon Hill, Dale Carnegie, and Emmet Fox, and had a direct influence on contemporary motivational writers such as Tony Robbins and Louise Hay.

Schooled in the Jesuit tradition, Murphy became increasingly interested in new experiences through the power of prayer, and eventually his studies turned his interest toward various Asian religions and Eastern philosophy. He went to India to pursue indepth study of all of the major faiths from the time of their beginning, and extended these studies to the great philosophers from ancient times until the present.

Murphy wrote more than thirty books, the most famous of which, *The Power of Your Subconscious Mind*, first published in 1963, became an international bestseller, with millions of copies sold worldwide. In the mid 1940s, he moved to Los Angeles, where he became minister of the Los Angeles Divine Science Church, which he built into one of the largest New Thought congregations in the country.

HAMPTON ROADS
PUBLISHING COMPANY

. . . for the evolving human spirit

Hampton Roads Publishing Company publishes books on a variety of subjects, including spirituality, health, and other related topics.

For a copy of our latest trade catalog, call (978) 465-0504 or visit our distributor's website at *www.redwheelweiser.com*. You can also sign up for our newsletter and special offers by going to *www.redwheelweiser.com/newsletter/*.